# finding rest

# finding rest

**Kent Sisco**

**Book Cover Design**
Ryan Sisco
Nathaniel Sisco
Suzanne Sisco

RIBOZUM PRESS
2016

Copyright © 2016 by Kent Sisco

All rights reserved. This book or any portion thereof may not be reproduced or used in any manner whatsoever without the express written permission of the publisher except for the use of brief quotations in a book review or scholarly journal.

Scripture quotations are from the ESV® Bible (The Holy Bible, English Standard Version®), copyright © 2001 by Crossway, a publishing ministry of Good News Publishers. Used by permission. All rights reserved.

First Printing: 2016

ISBN 978-1-329-90602-0

RIBOZUM PRESS
7447 Westerfield Road
Lynden, WA 98264

www.ribozumpress.com

Ordering Information:
Special discounts are available on quantity purchases by corporations, associations, educators, and others. For details, contact the publisher at the above listed address.

U.S. trade bookstores and wholesalers: Please contact RIBOZUM PRESS

Tel: (360) 739-5279 or email kent@ribozum.com.

# Dedication

To my wonderful wife (Suzanne) and family.

Thank you.

Without your support, encouragement, and patience, I would have never been able to get this first book looking and reading like a book should. I am looking forward to writing more books and reading each one of yours, as well.

# Contents

Acknowledgements ........................................................ ix
Preface ....................................................................... xi
Introduction ................................................................ 1
Chapter 1: Brief History of Languages ...................... 5
Chapter 2: Kanji from Biblical Accounts ................. 13
Chapter 3: Your Worldview Matters ....................... 28
Chapter 4: Allegory of the Gospel in Kanji ............. 32
Chapter 5: Is Man Basically Good? ......................... 35
Chapter 6: The Context of the Gospel .................... 46
Chapter 7: Peeking through the Veil ...................... 62
Chapter 8: The Burden that Man Carries ............... 68
Chapter 9: Thy Kingdom Come ............................... 76
Chapter 10: Invitation to Rest ................................ 88
Chapter 11: He is Our Righteousness ..................... 96
Conclusion: The Crossroad .................................... 109
Appendix ................................................................ 113
Notes ..................................................................... 115

# Acknowledgements

I would like to thank my wife, my family and parents without whose encouragement and help this book would never have been completed. It was my wife and my mom and dad who really spurred me on to write the book in the first place.

As this is my first book, I had no readership other than my family and parents. I am very thankful for their willingness to read through the manuscripts, some drafts numerous times, looking for passages that were confusing and coming up with ways and words to help clarify the message.

I am also thankful to my wife for coming up with such a great title for the book, "finding rest." Several titles had been proposed and they were all so good. In the end, it was really this title and my wife's design concepts that inspired the cover of the book that my sons, Nathaniel and Ryan, staged and produced which really captures the essence of what the book is about and clinched it for me.

Thank you so much!

# Preface

You might be wondering why I am writing a book about the gospel of Jesus Christ hidden in Japanese Kanji. (Kanji is the word that the Japanese use for Chinese symbols.) Well, one reason would be to show that words, with their meanings and symbols, can be adopted from one culture and incorporated into another and still hold their original meaning after thousands of years. In this case, in the 7th century, Chinese characters began to be used by Japanese scholars and statesmen for the purpose of chronicling history and codifying laws.

Another reason is that I spent a significant part of my childhood and early adult years as a missionary kid in Japan and learned to speak, read, and write Japanese. As I studied the strokes and symbols of these ancient Chinese characters, I discovered embedded within them concise keyword outlines of Biblical history which leads me to the most important reason for writing this book. Whenever the gospel is shared with Japanese people, the inevitable response is "Christianity is a Western religion," but is it?

Before we go on to look at the message of the gospel in Kanji, there is a caveat… although we may find parts and pieces of the gospel message embedded within many of the Kanji, it's important to note that we must not use these to derive the gospel message.

The gospel is clearly described in the Bible and we must always go back to Scripture to keep from straying from its narrative. Nothing supersedes the Word of God, not insights, not experiences, not Kanji with a Biblical message built in, not even an angel from heaven preaching another gospel.

> *"But even if we or an angel from heaven should preach to you a gospel contrary to the one we preached to you, let him be accursed."*
> *(Galatians 1:8)*

Twists and turns in the telling of stories can make a story much more interesting for the audience, but may introduce error in the message and lead people astray. Thus it's important to go back to the source and not rely entirely on what we find in man's interpretations.

Having said that, I hope you will enjoy this book as we delve into the gospel message we shall uncover in some of the thought provoking symbol combinations and collages that are found in the Kanji used in the Japanese language today.

## Introduction

I REMEMBER the very first day we arrived in Japan. I was 11 years old. It was the late fall of 1974. The air was crisp and cold as we stood on the platform at Ueno station for the very first time. I distinctly recall the feeling of wonder at the people and signs and sounds that were so different from what I was used to in Seattle. Over the loud speaker, a man's voice was saying something I couldn't understand. A train was just pulling out of the platform. I knew right then and there that I was entering a whole new world of amazing discovery. I can even now remember thinking I can't wait to interact with this new world.

On the platform, there was a small kiosk with newspapers with strange characters written all over them. There was hot tea in little clear plastic cups with thin metal handles. I also noticed unusual food and drink items I'd never seen before, including other things I didn't recognize all around the little shop. A net of mandarin oranges hanging in a net from a hook by the counter caught my eye and I asked my Dad if we could buy a bag. I looked at the coins he put in my hand 1, 5, 10, 50, and 100 yen coins which had Chinese characters on them. They looked so mysterious, especially the ones with little holes in the middle of them. What do these strange symbols mean? I thought to myself, "One day I am going to be able to read these characters."

As I walked up to the counter, I sensed a new kind of excitement that I had never experienced before. It was the beginning of a new adventure. The lady in the shop said something I couldn't understand and all I could do was point at the item I wanted. I put the coins on the counter and I watched as she picked each one up and put them in a shallow little round tray that had a thin rubber mat in it. Then she removed the coins for payment and handed me the net of oranges and then passed the tray back to me with the remaining coins. I took the bag and the coins from the tray. I had successfully negotiated my first transaction and in that moment I realized I had already begun to learn so much. I was determined to learn how to speak, read, and write Japanese so that I could make new friends and make Japan my new home.

A few months later, I began taking Japanese classes at Karuizawa Language School. I remember learning how to write hiragana and then numbers in Kanji. Then one day I was given an assignment to convert sentences written in romaji into hiragana and Kanji. I was given some examples to follow. That night, I was so excited to impress my teacher, I got out a Japanese dictionary and found all the Kanji I needed and wrote every sentence out as precisely as possible. When I brought the assignment to class I was so excited for my teacher to see it. She was amazed at what I had done. I was so proud of myself. I had written every sentence only using Kanji.

After she collected herself, and with all the patience and kindness she could possibly muster, she explained to me that Kanji not only had sounds, but they also had specific meanings. The Kanji I had selected were the wrong ones for each and every word in each of the sentences. The sentences I had written were completely unintelligible. After considerable explanation, I finally understood what the assignment was and what Kanji were to be used and where. It was a good lesson for me to learn. I wish I had a copy of my homework from back then to see what I'd actually written.

A few days later someone showed me the Kanji for "boat." They told me that the symbols in this Kanji coincided with the historical biblical record of Noah's Ark. The Kanji for "boat" actually has the number "eight" and "mouths" in it and there were 8 people on Noah's Ark, Noah and his wife, his three sons and their wives. I was amazed. How could that be? Not soon after, I was introduced to the Kanji for "righteousness" having the two parts depicting a "lamb" over "me." What an amazing picture for righteousness from a biblical perspective! I could hardly believe what I was seeing. I wanted to know if there were more Kanji that had a biblical meaning. If Kanji represented pictures of things and pictures represent a thousand words, could the words for other Kanji be explained from the Bible, too? Where should I go to find out? I thought, what better place to find Kanji with a biblical meaning than in the Bible itself. So, I began methodically reading the Bible in Japanese starting from the book of Matthew, a journey I will never forget.

I would like to take you on a small portion of that journey through a single verse in the book of Matthew as I saw it as a young man many years ago. The verse contains 4 individual Kanji that I believe paint a compelling picture of the gospel message as seen through the eyes of a child. The verse is Matthew 11:28.

*"Come to me, all who labor and are heavy laden, and I will give you rest."*

These are the words Jesus spoke with compassion, as only He could, truly knowing the plight of mankind and the salvation only He could provide.

The four Kanji in this verse are, "person," "burden," "come," and "rest". These four Kanji make up the four points I wish to cover in this book that I've entitled: "Finding Rest."

# Chapter 1: Brief History of Languages

THE BIBLE describes a cataclysmic event, a worldwide flood, that destroyed all mankind. Only Noah, his family, and the animals that God brought to Noah to repopulate the earth were spared in a large ship (which you can read about in Genesis 6:13-22). From this point after the flood, up until an event known as the "Tower of Babel," the descendants of Noah most likely communicated in one language.

The tower of Babel, as recorded in Genesis 11:1-9, is the event, after the flood, where all the people of the earth gathered together to make a name for themselves. They decided to build a tower to reach to the heavens. But God stopped them by confusing their speech and He dispersed them across the face of the earth.

> *"Therefore its name was called Babel, because there the Lord confused the language of all the earth. And from there the Lord dispersed them over the face of all the earth."*
> *(Genesis 11:9)*

confusion

The word, "confusion" used in the Japanese translation of Genesis 11:9 is made up of two Kanji, "mix" and "rebellion." This word describes the Tower of Babel event seen in the four symbols on the following page that make up the two Kanji.

After ① the flood, ② the descendants of Noah ③ gathered together and they ④ rebelled against God and he ⑤ confused their language and they spoke in ⑥ strange ⑦ tongues.

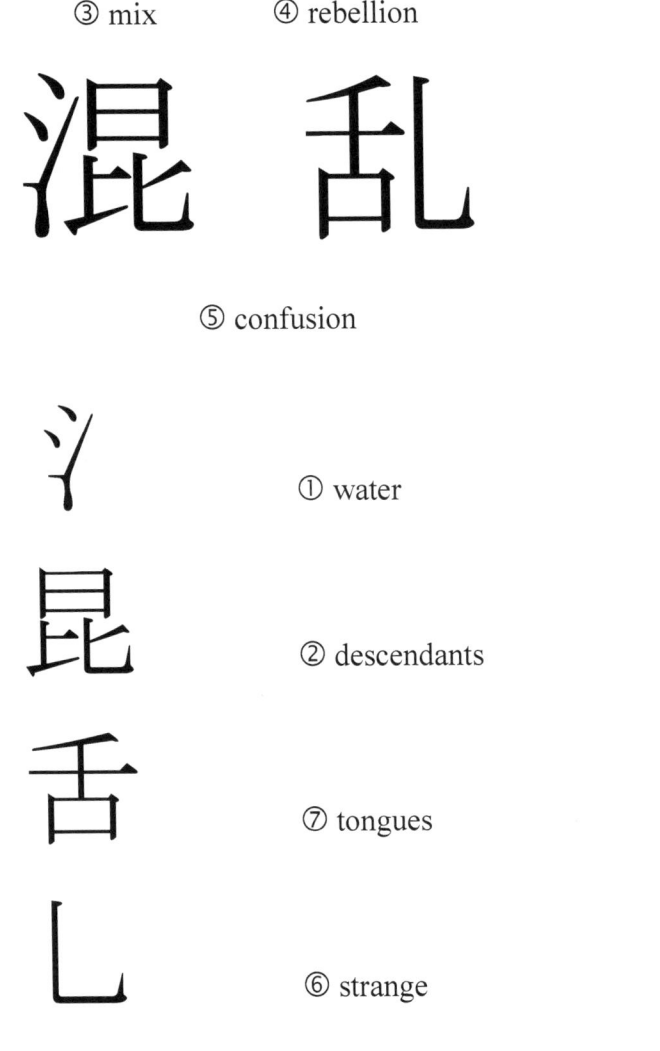

The people that were scattered throughout the world with their new God-given languages would have orally retained the historical record that preceded the dispersion, such as creation, wrongdoing, judgment, and the flood. Events following would have been injected as meaningful elements into the new cultures they began to establish. So it stands to reason that one might be able to find parts and pieces of recognizable Biblical history covering thousands of years embedded within cultures and languages around the world. This is the case with Chinese characters.

And yet, here we are today about 4,000 years after the tower of Babel and many linguistic scholars are looking at the hundreds of countries in the world with their respective multitude of ethnic groups, each with their own language, trying to piece together or figure out where all these languages came from.

Words and their meanings can come from one language and be used in another. Clearly we see words that we use today in the English language are derived from many other languages like Latin, Greek, French, German, Dutch, including a few words from Japanese. And Japanese language speakers know that Chinese, Japanese, and Koreans share thousands of the same words. Even the Japanese phonetic symbols, hiragana and katakana, are simplified forms of their more complex Chinese phonetic symbols from which they were borrowed.

There are over 6,000 languages on earth today with over 1,500 of them still having no written form. The Biblical account of God confusing the languages of man at the Tower of Babel makes some sense.

The written form of the Chinese language began to develop some 3,000 years ago and about 1,500 years later the Japanese acquired Chinese characters in order to advance their education and culture. While there are as many as 20,000 plus Chinese characters, a college level student in China needs to know only the first 4,000 in its ordered list, to be functionally literate.

In Japan, students need to have learned 2,136 (Jouyou) Kanji in order to enter college. This may seem like a lot to learn, but there are tricks to learning these quickly and retaining them. In fact, once you learn the first 1000, you can just about sound out a Japanese newspaper. If you don't speak Japanese however, you won't understand the meaning of all the characters you are sounding out.

Chinese characters or "Kanji" (in Japanese) are essentially strokes that make up symbols that represent pictures of things, concepts, or abstracts which we call characters. Each symbol has a sound or two associated with it. In the Chinese language, there are generally one or two sounds per symbol.

Because the Japanese spoken language existed before the adoption of Chinese characters, the Japanese mapped their own sounds to the adopted characters. They also incorporated Chinese words, as is, with the "Chinese sounds" for these symbols which accounts for the more than two readings per symbol in the Japanese language. It can be phenomenally confusing when you first start learning to read Chinese characters or "Kanji".

person

For example, the "Chinese readings" for the word, "person," in Japanese are "JIN" and "NIN," however the Chinese themselves read it as "REN." The Japanese reading of this character on the other hand is "hito." For the most part, the rule is whenever a Kanji is standing by itself in a Japanese sentence, you would pronounce it using the Japanese reading. In this case, you would read it, "hito." If it is next to another Kanji, then you would use the appropriate Chinese reading.

person

Very few characters actually represent the shape of an object as in the character for "person" above. If you were to draw a stick-figured man and erased the head and arms, you would have the remaining shape that looks like the legs of a person. This was enough of a symbol to describe "person." People are different from animals in this outward appearance because they walk around on two legs all the time. Now whenever you see this shape, you'll think "person."

mouth

Another character that represents, in part, an actual object is the symbol for "mouth" which has a Chinese reading of "KOU" and "KU" and a Japanese reading of "kuchi." Again, if you were to draw a "squarish" stick figure of the face of a person talking or opening their mouth to eat something and then erased all the other facial elements leaving only the mouth, you would have the symbol for the word, "mouth."

mouth

These two characters (person and mouth) when placed beside each other are read using the Chinese sounds, "JINKOU" which means, "population". Why? I don't know, but two major considerations when dealing with a population are feeding and communicating, and both use the mouth. In the Bible, there is a story about the feeding of the 5,000 and the problem that Jesus' disciples soon recognized with the large multitude (or population) following Jesus around was that they were going to go hungry if they were not told to leave.

> *"Now when it was evening, the disciples came to him and said, 'This is a desolate place, and the day is now over; send the crowds away to go into the villages and buy food for themselves.'"*
> *(Matthew 14:15)*

You can read more about this story in Matthew 14:13-21, Mark 6:31-44, Luke 9:10-17 and John 6:5-15.

人口

population

I am not saying that the word for "population" comes from this story in the Bible. I am simply using it as an illustration. This story does clearly represent logistical issues with large numbers of people having to do with the mouth (communication, food) that any society would understand. The Chinese might have used this logic and put the two Kanji together, "people" and "mouth," in order to describe the word "population" in this way.

混乱

confusion

I am suggesting however, that the word, "confusion", as I explained at the beginning of this chapter does come directly from the historical record of the Tower of Babel as described in the Bible.

*Note: From here on out in this book, excluding the numbers 1 to 10 on the next page, I will be showing various kanji with their respective symbol combinations that bring to mind the biblical historical record.*

The characters below represent the numbers 1 to 10 in Chinese characters.

一 二 三 四 五
六 七 八 九 十

Clearly the first three in this list show a physical count of strokes for the numbers they represent. The number 1 has one stroke. The number 2 has two strokes, and 3, three strokes. When you look at the remaining symbols though, the number is no longer physically represented by the number of strokes. They are just symbols that represent these numbers. Most Chinese characters are not "stick-figured" pictures of the things they represent, they are just symbols with a specific order of strokes.

The order in which each stroke is written for each symbol is very important. In fact, it's the order in which the strokes are written that help the writer remember the meanings of the symbols and the stories that are used to remember them. In this book, we will not go into the stroke order for each Kanji. Just accept for now that each symbol in its simplest form is generally recognizable in the Kanji examples I will be sharing throughout this book. Also note that individual symbols do not change their meaning. Once you learn a symbol or kanji such as the kanji/symbol for person, whenever you see it in another kanji, it always means person.

# Chapter 2: Kanji from Biblical Accounts

AS WE saw in the first chapter, the word, "confusion" is made up of two Kanji, "mix" and "rebellion." Let's now take a look at some more Kanji that have Biblical historical meaning embedded in their symbols.

Symbols are made up of strokes and then often combined with other symbols to form more complex looking characters for words as in the Kanji for "ship". This brings us back to my opening paragraph in chapter 1 about the worldwide flood and the large ship that God told Noah to build. Even though Christianity is supposedly a "Western" religion, Westerners may not know how many people were aboard Noah's ark unless they have read the historical record found in the Bible. However, if I were to ask a Chinese or Japanese person how many people were on Noah's Ark and told them that the answer can be found in the word for "ship", their answer would be, "eight people". Why is that?

ship

The single Chinese character for "ship" is made up of three other characters representing three distinct words "boat", "eight", and "mouth" as depicted in the following three characters. The symbol on the left side is the Kanji for "boat". Used by itself, it represents small boat, but when combined with the Kanji "eight" and "mouths," it means "ship". The first large ship in recorded human history is found in the Bible in Genesis 6, which is the biblical record of Noah's Ark. It was large enough to hold all the animals God brought to Noah and many hundreds of people. It was a very large ship with three decks.

So how many people were actually on Noah's Ark?

Well, according to the Biblical account, the only people aboard this ship were Noah and his wife and his three sons and their wives. That adds up to eight people, a 人口 "JINKOU" (population) of eight people on board. You can see why a person that reads Chinese characters might know the answer to that question right off the bat. Now you can see that, too!

It's easy to imagine how the symbols in the character for "ship," written down in Chinese 3,000 years ago, might have been introduced from the oral history of Noah's Ark, an event that happened 1,000 years earlier. The people at the tower of Babel would have known the story of Noah's Ark as it had just occurred a hundred years earlier.

It's likely that other cultures around the world would have versions of this same story, as well. Chinese isn't the only language influenced by the Bible, there are many idioms that we use in English that come directly from the Bible, too.

  ship

  boat

  eight

  mouths

Just as the translation of the Bible into German by Martin Luther had an influence on the German language, the historical record delivered through the translation of the King James Bible influenced the development of the English language.

An example of an idiom or "picture" we use in English that comes directly from the Bible is the phrase, "a wolf in sheep's clothing", which comes from a warning in the Bible from the book of Matthew.

> *"Beware of false prophets, who come to you in sheep's clothing but inwardly are ravenous wolves."*
> *(Matthew 7:15)*

Many people who speak English know exactly what we mean when we use this "picture" idiom, "a wolf in sheep's clothing", but they may not know that it comes directly from this statement that Jesus makes.

The idea that someone would try to appear like a sheep, so that they could make others think they were harmless and deceive them, only makes sense when you understand it from the Bible. In nature, wolves never deceive sheep by wearing sheep skins. But throughout the Bible, man is likened to sheep.

> *"All we like sheep have gone astray; we have turned—every one—to his own way; and the Lord has laid on him the iniquity of us all."*
> *(Isaiah 53:6)*

And by inference in the famous psalm of David,

*"The LORD is my shepherd; I shall not want."*
*(Psalm 23:1)*

A person who is inwardly a ravening wolf, but acts on the outside like "one of the fold," might be able to deceive others and the "sheep" wouldn't even know it, even when they are standing right next to them.

There are many false religions, too many to count, conjured up by false prophets in the world that have left so many people deceived.

In Japan, a religion that causes lots of confusion, devised by false prophets, is Shinto-ism. The Shinto religion teaches that there are an infinite number of gods. They call this, "Yaoyorozu no kami", directly translated meaning, "8 million gods." This is the belief that "god is in everything" and thus there are many gods. There are gods for everything in nature such as streams, bamboo groves, waterfalls, and of course stones. There are gods for every manufactured thing including things like toilets.

Throughout the Bible however, God is distinguished from His handiwork and the Bible teaches us that He alone is God.

How will people learn about the one and only creator God of the Bible?

*How then will they call on him in whom they have not believed? And how are they to believe in him of whom they have never heard? And how are they to hear without someone preaching?"*
*(Romans 10:14)*

deceitful

There is a Kanji that has the meaning "pretend, feign, false, deceitful" which has the symbols, "person" and "sheep," which you'd think would be the meaning for shepherd, but it carries the meaning of the warning in Matthew 7:15.

Could this "person" standing next to the sheep be a picture of each and every one of the many false prophets that Jesus was cautioning about? I believe it is.

Symbols in Chinese characters are parts of stories as we can see here. Children in Japan are taught stories to remember the symbols that make up these Kanji. They are taught stories, but not the historical record that we have from the Bible. The Japanese people need to hear the biblical record and someone needs to tell them.

Japan needs bold Christians to share the good news of the Gospel from the Bible. Even though we will encounter some very intriguing characters and symbols throughout this book that reflect the biblical record, the Kanji by themselves are not sufficient enough to convey the message God has for the world. These symbols need to be expressed in light of God's Word.

deceitful

person, man

sheep

I believe we can see the historical record found in the Bible had a profound influence on the development of Chinese characters that the Japanese later adopted. The gospel message was already being embedded in the Chinese characters (Kanji) long before the West was converted to Christianity.

In this next example, once again most non-Christian Westerners might not know the answer to the question I am about to ask regarding the central religious practice of "sacrifice" found throughout the Old Testament. But if I was to show the typical Japanese junior high school student the Kanji for "sacrifice," even though they may have no knowledge of the Bible at all, they would know the answer to my question.

But first let me point out that in Japan, there are legends of human sacrifice, "hitobashira," translated as "human pillar," where young maidens were buried alive at the base of new construction sites. This was a sacrifice to appease the gods and to protect the construction against any type of destruction.

The symbols that make up the Kanji for "sacrifice," however, do not refer to human sacrifice as seen in historical Japanese culture, instead they originate in Hebrew culture.

Let's look at the word "sacrifice" and its symbols that would have had its origins in an event that spread throughout the known world and made its way into China in 950 BC when the Chinese also were performing human sacrifice.

*Note: human sacrifice was performed by burying people alive.*

sacrifice

Throughout the Old Testament there are various entries that record both human and animal sacrifices. The Israelites in the Bible were commanded by God to offer animal sacrifices, even though other kingdoms around the world at that time, as recorded in the Bible, were practicing human sacrifice.

*Note: There are times, even in Old Testament Israel, when human sacrifice was performed, but these were never performed as a rite in obedience to a commandment of God.*

So let's ask a Japanese junior high school student to look at the Kanji for sacrifice.

What is sacrificed?

犧

sacrifice

牛     oxen

羊     sheep

Their answer would be "**oxen**" and "**sheep**".

You can see on the left hand side of the Kanji there is the Kanji for oxen and on the top right hand side we see the Kanji for sheep.

> *"Solomon offered as peace offerings to the Lord 22,000 oxen and 120,000 sheep. So the king and all the people of Israel dedicated the house of the Lord." (1 Kings 8:63.)*

If you know your Bible, you might have known the answer right off the bat, but most people in the West don't, even though Christianity is a supposedly a "Western" religion.

Solomon was well-known throughout the earth, as it states in 1 Kings 4:34

> *"And people of all nations came to hear the wisdom of Solomon, and from all the kings of the earth, who had heard of his wisdom."*

The dedication of the temple, at which the 22,000 oxen and 120,000 sheep were sacrificed, was an event in which all Israel participated.

This event would have been announced throughout the populated world at the time due to Solomon's worldwide fame. The prayer of Solomon states that the purpose of the dedication and the sacrifice was,

*"that all the peoples of the earth may know that the Lord is God; there is no other."*
*(1 Kings 8:60)*

There is a third Kanji however, found in the word for "sacrifice," and it is the following.

What meaning does this Kanji in the word for sacrifice have?

Why wouldn't a Japanese person include this as one of the things being sacrificed?

These two symbols are connected and should be seen as the picture of a hand holding a spear. Thus it would be the one performing the sacrifice and not the one being sacrificed. It therefore implies "the executioner."

我

*[the executioner]*

*Note: Later in this book, we'll get back to the actual meaning of this Kanji as the Japanese use it today.*

手     hand

戈     spear

As a side note, the Kanji for sheep is also the same Kanji used in the words for ram, goat, and lamb.

| 牡羊 | 牡 | 羊 |
|---|---|---|
| ram | male animal | sheep |

| 山羊 | 山 | 羊 |
|---|---|---|
| goat | mountain | sheep |

| 小羊 | 小 | 羊 |
|---|---|---|
| lamb | small, little | sheep |

The Kanji for "sacrifice" would also include a reference to the sacrifice offered when Solomon was anointed King of Israel.

> *"And they offered sacrifices to the Lord, and on the next day offered burnt offerings to the Lord, 1,000 bulls, 1,000 rams, and 1,000 lambs, with their drink offerings, and sacrifices in abundance for all Israel."*
> *(1 Chronicles 29:21)*

The Kanji for sacrifice would include all of the bull, ram, goat, and lamb sacrifices that were offered in Israel until Christ became the final sacrificial lamb.

So, if there are Kanji that happen to have pictures of biblical history in them, why aren't the Japanese as a whole more receptive to the gospel?

The more important questions may be, why aren't they asking who is this God who required such a sacrifice and why did He require it? Remember the purpose was...

> *"that all the peoples of the earth may know that the Lord is God; there is no other."*
> *(1 Kings 8:60)*

# Chapter 3: Your Worldview Matters

> *"But we preach Christ crucified, unto the Jews a stumbling block, and unto the Greeks foolishness;"*
> *(1 Corinthians 1:23, King James Version)*

WHAT YOU have been taught and what you know make a difference in how you respond to the gospel message found in the Bible. The message, "we preach Christ crucified", results in two different responses based on the unique cultures of these ethnic groups, Jews and Gentiles. Why a stumbling block to Jews and why foolishness to Gentiles? These responses are based predominately on their worldview, what they believe about the world and what they believe about man.

The Jews have a reference point to God, creation, man, sin, judgment, sacrifice, atonement, and the Messiah, but Jesus did not fit the description of who they believed the Messiah would be.

> *"Jesus said to them, 'Truly, truly, I say to you, before Abraham was, I am.' So they picked up stones to throw at him, but Jesus hid himself and went out of the temple."*
> *(John 8:58, 59)*

They took offense at Him and His words because this is the very name God used when He commanded Moses to lead the Israelites out of Egypt.

*"God said to Moses, 'I am who I am.' And he said, 'Say this to the people of Israel, "I am has sent me to you."'" (Exodus 3:14)*

The Gentiles have a different reference point to gods (or no god at all) and to the origin of man, wrongdoing and judgment, so this message doesn't fit into their worldview, especially in this day when Evolution is taught with an emphasis that "there is no God." It just doesn't make any sense.

When people are taught that there is no God and that man evolved, the idea of a need for a Savior, "Christ crucified," makes absolutely no sense and appears foolish.

When you share the gospel message with the Japanese, because they have significant long-held traditions in Buddhism and Shintoism, they are aware that there is a spirit world. But they may simply respond with "Christianity is a Western religion" because they have no background from which to understand the message, even though it's right in front of them, embedded in their everyday language as we shall soon see. What's even more interesting though is that the Japanese wholeheartedly believe another truly Western theory, a system of faith to which is ascribed supreme importance, called Evolution, only recently popularized in Japan through Western Europe by Charles Darwin.

The theory of Evolution is taught as fact and based on random, continuous, and uniform processes that take millions of years. According to the theory and "teaching" of Evolution, there is no life after death, there is just the here and now. The proponents of this theory insist that man, as he evolved, created the need for God. While Darwin never emphatically denied religion, his successors certainly have.

The worldview of Evolution is a belief system that requires faith. Why is it a belief system? The theory of Evolution is made up of conclusions on the basis of incomplete information and it requires belief in things that cannot be proved. Admittedly, the existence of God also cannot be proved, but requires faith.

In a country like Japan, that deeply believes in the spirit world as well, how is the spiritual world accounted for in this Evolution equation?

It's all very confusing when you have a worldview that is primarily based on Evolutionary thought and then intermingled with religion. So you can see how "preaching Christ crucified" is foolishness to the Japanese. In order to understand the gospel message people need Biblical context.

There is one passage in the Bible that I'd like to use as the centerpiece for the gospel found in Japanese Kanji. The verses we shall use describe why Jesus was a stumbling block to the Jews and why by itself it looks like foolishness to Gentiles. With a closer look at these verses all people can come to an understanding of the gospel message and how it applies directly to them.

> *"Come to me, all who labor and are heavy laden, and I will give you rest. Take my yoke upon you, and learn from me, for I am gentle and lowly in heart, and you will find rest for your souls. For my yoke is easy, and my burden is light."*
> *(Matthew 11:28 -30)*

These words were spoken by Jesus Christ relate to the man-made laws, rules and regulations that the spiritual leaders in Israel at that time imposed on people for the sake of making themselves "appear" more acceptable in the sight of God. These rules were heavy burdens on people. Jesus was saying, "come learn from Me and you'll find rest for your souls in a way that is not putting heavy burdens on you." The Jewish leaders found Jesus a stumbling block because He discredited their man-made impositions (legalism), and because of this the leaders retaliated claiming that Jesus was a blasphemer and not who He said He was. The Jewish leaders told the people that Jesus was not the Messiah, so the people found Jesus to be a stumbling block and they eventually put Him to death.

The Jews had all the context in the world to understand the reason for a Messiah. They had the background teaching of one Creator God who created the world and all that is in it, including mankind. They were not believers of evolution and they certainly did not believe that man was here on the planet by chance.

We can see how these words of Jesus' also apply to the burden of sin we carry as we become aware of God's law and begin to realize our guilt as we read the Bible. We know that we are condemned before God, and need a Savior.

# Chapter 4: Allegory of the Gospel in Kanji

*"Come to me, all who labor and are heavy laden, and I will give you rest."*
*(Matthew 11:28)*

THESE WORDS of Jesus, from the Word of God, encapsulate the gospel message succinctly, especially so when we look at it through the pictures described by the Kanji, found in this verse.

"すべて、疲れた 人 、重 荷 を負っている人は、わたしのところに 來 なさい。わたしがあなたがたを 休 ませてあげます。"

Matthew 11:28

I will use the four Kanji from this verse, that I have placed boxes around, to help paint a picture of the gospel. I will also use other supporting Kanji to further clarify the gospel message. In doing so, I think we will see what a great picture of the gospel the Japanese actually have in their own written language borrowed from the Chinese.

Again, these Kanji are not enough by themselves without the Word of God. It's God's Word that sheds light on what these "pictures" or Kanji mean.

> *"Come to me, all who labor and are heavy laden, and I will give you rest." (Matthew 11:28 -30)*

| 人 | 荷 | 來 | 休 |
|---|---|---|---|
| person | burden | come | rest |

The three symbols below all represent "man" or "person". They mean exactly the same thing, it's just that the shape changes based on the position in which the symbol for "man" is placed in each Kanji.

Take a moment to find the symbol for man in each of the four Kanji above.

| 人 | 亻 | 人 |
|---|---|---|
| person, man | person, man | person, man |

John Bunyan, the writer of Pilgrim's Progress, paints a picture of a young man who by the reading of the Bible, becomes convicted of his sins and his need to be freed from his burden.

The young man feels the weight of this unbearable burden so much so that people around him can see his distress and they tell him to just let it go, but he doesn't know how to lay the burden down. In his home town he fortunately meets a man who shows him the way to begin his journey to the place of deliverance and onward toward the celestial city.

Along his journey to deliverance from his burden, he is misled by deceivers and runs into various troubles. But he is brought back by a man who directs him back onto the path of deliverance.

The place of deliverance in this story is the Cross. As soon as he approaches it, the burden strapped to him is released from him and it rolls away and is no more.

Pilgrim's Progress is an allegory, a picture of a person who becomes aware of their condition in the sight of God and desires to get right with God through God's solution and finds rest for his soul. We can see this same story unfolding in the Kanji that we are highlighting from the verse in Matthew 11:28.

Even though there are images of man's condition and pictures of the good news hidden in the characters that the Japanese use every day, without the Bible, there is no understanding and no conviction.

The premise of this book is that these symbols for man represent specific people, both historical and present day figures, events and locations within the narrative of the gospel. We are about to discover who they are and where they are from.

# Chapter 5: Is Man Basically Good?

SOME PEOPLE believe that man is basically good, they might say, "What do I need God for anyway? I'm accountable to no one, I decide what's right and wrong for me."

But, if there is a God, and we are truly accountable to Him, wouldn't He instruct us as to what is right and wrong? And wouldn't you want to know what those instructions are?

The Bible says that the heart of man is desperately wicked. It was for this reason that God brought judgment in the form of the worldwide flood during Noah's day.

> *"The Lord saw that the wickedness of man was great in the earth, and that every intention of the thoughts of his heart was only evil continually."*
> *(Genesis 6:5)*

悪

evil

Even after the flood, man's heart really didn't change. We see this in a Scripture written more than 1,700 years after the flood.

> *"The heart is deceitful above all things, and desperately sick: who can understand it?"*
> *(Jeremiah 17:9)*

The Kanji for "evil", as you see below, contains the symbol for "heart" in it.

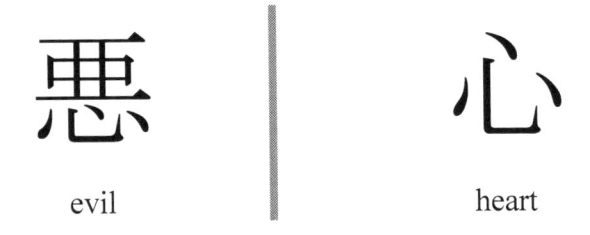

悪 | 心

evil | heart

So let's look at a few of the Kanji that have the symbol for heart in them to see what man realized about himself when these words were first described thousands of years ago. I have compiled a short list, but there are close to a hundred more that paint the heart of man in a negative light.

| 心 | 忄 | 小 |
|---|---|---|
| heart, mind | heart, mind | heart, mind |

| 忏 | 怪 | 㥘 |
|---|---|---|
| stubborn | suspicious | foolish |
| 怯 | 恨 | 怏 |
| cowardly | malicious | grudging |
| 恊 | 悍 | 恪 |
| threatening | repulsive | stingy |
| 悁 | 惜 | 惨 |
| impatience | disappointing | wretched |
| 悽 | 懈 | 悔 |
| sorrowful | laziness | lament |
| 愎 | 愴 | 慢 |
| disobedient | pathetic | ridicule |

| | | |
|---|---|---|
| 慘 cruel | 憤 indignant | 憾 remorse |
| 惱 torment | 忌 abominable | 忿 anger |
| 恣 selfish | 怠 neglect | 悄 anxiety |
| 懼 dread | 悚 fear | 怨 resentment |
| 恥 shame | 惡 evil | 惑 delusion |
| 悶 agony | 慾 covetousness | 惷 confusion |
| 憎 hate | 慙 humiliated | and many, many more |

When we look at all these Kanji with the symbol for "heart" in them, it paints a telling picture of the condition of man's heart. Of course there are Kanji with the symbol of "heart" in them that are good words too, like the word for "love" that has heart at its center.

愛

love

However, the Japanese rarely use this word to say, "I love you." It's far too strong a word. More often in Japanese the word used would be "like." But in the Bible this is the Kanji that is used in the verse,

"... *God is love..." (1 John 4:16b)*

There are other words too, such as grace and mercy which contain the symbol of heart in them and it's right that it be there, because deep in our hearts we can recognize grace and mercy because our eyes were opened to see good and evil. Even so, it is easier for us to exhibit anger, wrath, malice, slander rather than grace, mercy, and love.

恵み

grace

憐れみ

mercy

Colossians 3 admonishes us to put on the new self and lay aside the old self with its evil practices.

> "Put to death therefore what is earthly in you: sexual immorality, impurity, passion, evil desire, and covetousness, which is idolatry. On account of these the wrath of God is coming. In these you too once walked, when you were living in them. But now you must put them all away: anger, wrath, malice, slander, and obscene talk from your mouth. Do not lie to one another, seeing that you have put off the old self with its practices and have put on the new self, which is being renewed in knowledge after the image of its creator."
> (Colossians 3:5-10)

I believe that the Kanji with the symbol of "heart" in them are man's best assessment of the true nature of himself. The Bible more clearly states,

> "as it is written: 'None is righteous, no, not one;'" (Romans 3:10)

After World War II, a famous hymn, "What a friend we have in Jesus," was re-introduced to the Japanese by Christian missionaries. It quickly became popular with the Japanese people. Over the years the lyrics were lost as the popular culture embraced the tune by itself. Now known by many different titles, it is simply a recognizable melody without its original lyrics and therefore has lost its meaning. The Kanji, like this song need their original meaning restored.

答

sin, wrongdoing

In Japanese, one of the titles for the hymn mentioned above is "Tsumitoga wo ninou", which literally means "bearing sins". Within this title is the word "TOGA" which is the word for sin or wrongdoing. Let's look at its symbols. The word for wrongdoing has the symbols for "every" and "person" in it. The symbol for "person" is tiny in comparison to the symbol for "every." The emphasis here is on the symbol for "every", as in ALL people. Every person is guilty of wrongdoing.

God is very clear about this in His Word.

*"for all have sinned and fall short of the glory of God," (Romans 3:23)*

# 咎

sin, wrongdoing

各     every

人     person

Ayako Miura, a well-known writer in Japan, wrote a novel called "Shiokari Pass," an international best seller based on the true story of a young railway worker in northern Japan in the late eighteen hundreds. The young man in the novel, given the name Nobuo Nagano, finds himself confronted by a Christian evangelist, who challenges him to see if he can obey the words of the Bible,

> "... 'you shall love your neighbor as yourself.'"
> *(Leviticus 19:18, Mark 12:31)*

Nobuo, believing himself capable of great good, finds an opportunity to show compassion and kindness and love towards a fellow worker who was fired after having been caught stealing on the job. Nobuo decides to go to the station foreman and plead on behalf of his co-worker to have the young man's job restored to him saying, "If he steals again, you can fire me too."

The station foreman is so overcome by Nobuo's gesture, that he not only re-instates the young man, but gives him a new position in the company in another city so that he can have a new start. There is one condition, Nobuo would have to move to that city and work at the same location, too. This Nobuo does as he feels an obligation to his co-worker even though he would be moving away from his loved ones.

It's only a matter of time and Nobuo's co-worker begins to distrust his motives and accuses Nobuo of using him to make himself look better in the eyes of others. Nobuo maintains his calm, but on the inside begins to despise his co-worker, resenting him because he doesn't appreciate the sacrifice Nobuo has made to help him.

Not long after, Nobuo realizes that, while on the outside he appears to be a good deed doer to his fellow man, he is a hypocrite.

He begins to recognize that the sin of pride and hatred toward his neighbor is clearly seen by God and he begins to feel conviction in his heart.

The grace we may so easily extend to ourselves over and over when we sin is not so easily given to our neighbor who sins against us. As sinful man we have our limitations. But loving your neighbor is not just a nice thing to do, it is a command. And it is a command that comes directly from the Creator of heaven and earth. In fact, Jesus describes the kind of love we need to have when He says,

*"But I say to you, love your enemies and pray for those who persecute you,"*
*(Matthew 5:44)*

I do not want to give away the story as it's told in the novel, "Shiokari Pass", so I'll stop here, but I do recommend the book and the movie.

We've taken a look at what ancient Chinese civilization thought about man through some of the Kanji with the heart of man in them. We've also taken a look at an example from a Japanese novel of what modern man thinks of himself. It's now time to look at the context of where man finds himself in light of the narrative of the Bible.

So, let's jump in and take a look.

# Chapter 6: The Context of the Gospel

## Creation

WHO IS man in light of creation and the Biblical narrative?

> *"In the beginning God created the heavens and the earth." (Genesis 1:1)*

The Bible tells us that God **spoke** saying, "Let there be..." (Genesis 1: 2-31) and He created everything in six days.

> *"And God saw everything that he had made, and behold, it was very good. And there was evening and there was morning, the sixth day."*
> *(Genesis 1:31)*

And God created man and told man what to do.

> *"So God created man in his own image, in the image of God he created him; male and female he created them. And God blessed them. And God said to them, 'Be fruitful and multiply and fill the earth and subdue it, and have dominion over the fish of the sea and over the birds of the heavens and over every living thing that moves on the earth.'"*
> *(Genesis 1:27, 28)*

Everything functioned and moved in a way that God ordained. We see in the world an orderly design that **"walks"** in a manner that God designed it and **spoke** it into existence to do.

造

create

告

speak, announce

辶

walk

This same symbol for "walk" is also used in Kanji that represent things that the Bible teaches us that God set in place, as I will show in a moment. This symbol for "walk" not only refers to mankind or animals walking and moving about the face of the earth, it is also used in the word for a calendar "week". God spoke and all things "walk" or move as God first created it, even our calendar.

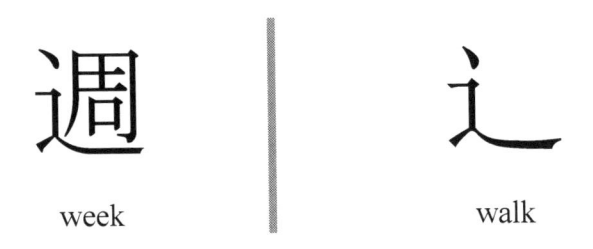

週　｜　辶

week　　　walk

In Genesis chapter 2, it tells us that on the seventh day God rested from all His work.

*"And on the seventh day God finished his work that he had done, and he rested on the seventh day from all his work that he had done." (Genesis 2:2)*

The entire world economy works off of a seven day week. This seven day week was established by God when He created and spoke the world into existence. The week is how we walk out our lives and this week has been repeated over and over since creation.

God also set in motion the planets in their respective "orbits". God spoke and everything was perfectly laid out to follow the instructions God gave and "it was very good." (Genesis 1:31)

# 軌道
orbit

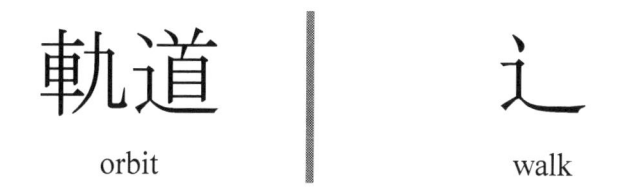

# 辶
walk

God also commanded Adam to walk a path of obedience. God gave man the choice to obey,

> *"And the Lord God commanded the man, saying, 'You may surely eat of every tree of the garden, but of the tree of the knowledge of good and evil you shall not eat, for in the day that you eat of it you shall surely die.'"*
> *(Genesis 2:16-17)*

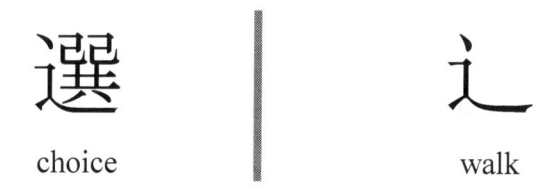

# 選
choice

# 辶
walk

There was also another tree in the garden and it was the "Tree of Life." If they ate of it, they would live forever. (Genesis 3:22-24)

God gave man a free will to make choices. There are two ways that man can walk. They can walk in the path of obedience or they can choose disobedience. God gave man a choice when He created the universe, a choice given to them in the garden in which they were placed.

# Deception

In the garden, there was a serpent who was more crafty than any of the wild animals as is told us in Genesis 3.

> *"Now the serpent was more crafty than any other beast of the field that the Lord God had made. He said to the woman, "Did God actually say, 'You shall not eat of any tree in the garden'?" And the woman said to the serpent, "We may eat of the fruit of the trees in the garden, but God said, 'You shall not eat of the fruit of the tree that is in the midst of the garden, neither shall you touch it, lest you die.'" But the serpent said to the woman, 'You will not surely die. For God knows that when you eat of it your eyes will be opened, and you will be like God, knowing good and evil.'"*
> *(Genesis 3:4, 5)*

The serpent was cunning and had already worked out a plan of deception when he approaches the woman to question her about what God had said.

The serpent's strategy is clearly depicted in the character meaning "to work out a plan of deception, to dupe, or conspire".

The three distinct parts (declare, tempting, tree) to the right read as though they came straight out of the Biblical record of the serpent deceiving Eve, telling her tempting words about the tree.

The serpent used enticing words to deceive the woman into eating of the fruit of the tree of the knowledge of good and evil and she shared it with her husband who was with her and they ate it. The serpent had worked out a plan of deception to take them in by saying that if they ate the "fruit" they would be like God.

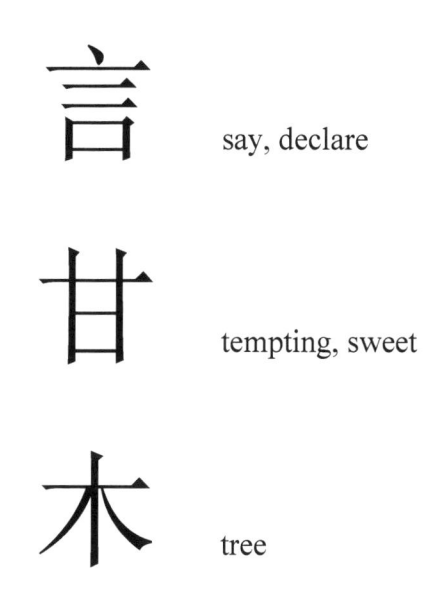

謀

plan of deception

言 say, declare

甘 tempting, sweet

木 tree

# Delusion

The serpent enticed the woman and she was tempted by his words and allowed herself to become deluded into thinking that these words were truth and that she would be like God just as the serpent had said. The word for delusion in Japanese is "MOUSOU," which is a compound word formed by two Kanji.

The reality is that death hangs over the woman if she eats from the tree of the knowledge of good and evil. She is warned not to eat from it by God (Genesis 2:16-17), but

> *"So when the woman saw that the tree was good for food, and that it was a delight to the eyes, and that the tree was to be desired to make one wise, she took of its fruit and ate, and she also gave some to her husband who was with her, and he ate."*
> *(Genesis 3:6)*

From our viewpoint, looking at the symbols in the word for "delusion", you can almost see yourself transported back there to the place where she stands in front of the tree. We can see that death looms over her and we want to shout out and say "Don't eat it!" But how many times have we personally found ourselves at this very spot, at a crossroads? And looking back now, you wish you'd chosen life.

Man always has a choice. The man and the woman have a choice here. And they chose to disobey… and sin entered the world.

deluded　　idea

# 妄想

delusion

亡 — perish

女 — woman

木 — tree

目 — eyes

心 — heart

## Decay

When the man and woman disobeyed God and ate of the fruit of the tree of the knowledge of good and evil, their bodies started down the path to decay. This was the last time man would have access to the tree of life in the garden of Eden. The Kanji for decay is made up of three symbols, "tree", "one", and "enclosure". The tree of life was soon to be closed off to them.

There is a phrase in Japanese ("kuchihateru") which translated means, "to die in obscurity" or "to decay completely" and it looks like this:

朽果てる

The first Kanji means, "decay" and the second is the word for "fruit". This second Kanji for "fruit" also means "to die". When Adam and Eve ate the fruit of the tree they were "enlightened," knowing good and evil, but now they would no longer have access to the tree of Life. They would be blocked from any access to it and they would die.

decay　　fruit, to die

# 朽果

to decay completely

木　tree

一　one

勹　enclosure

# 果

fruit, to die, enlightenment

In Buddhism, the Kanji used for "enlightenment" is this second Kanji for "fruit". If they only knew what this "fruit of enlightenment" leads to. The description of the fruit of the tree of the knowledge of good and evil was something that Satan said would enlighten but God said would lead to death. The Kanji for "fruit" in Japanese carries these meanings and is thus a reminder to us all.

All men will die and decay, but there is one who will never undergo decay. By the end of this book, we will see who this is.

When Eve eats of the tree of the knowledge of good and evil, and the man, Adam takes and eats of it too, in that very moment, their eyes were opened and they realized they were naked.

> "Then the eyes of both were opened, and they knew that they were naked. And they sewed fig leaves together and made themselves loincloths. And they heard the sound of the Lord God walking in the garden in the cool of the day, and the man and his wife hid themselves from the presence of the Lord God among the trees of the garden."
> (Genesis 3:7-8)

The immediate outcome in their hearts for their disobedience was **shame** and they hid themselves from God when they, with their physical **ears**, heard Him walking in the garden.

恥

shame

耳

ears

心

heart, mind

# Eviction

God banished Adam and Eve from the garden and drove them out so that they would not be able to eat from the tree of life and live forever. Because we are of Adam's race, we suffer the same fate.

> *"Then the Lord God said, "Behold, the man has become like one of us in knowing good and evil. Now, lest he reach out his hand and take also of the tree of life and eat, and live forever—" therefore the Lord God sent him out from the garden of Eden to work the ground from which he was taken. He drove out the man, and at the east of the garden of Eden he placed the cherubim and a flaming sword that turned every way to guard the way to the tree of life." (Genesis 3:22-24)*

The colloquial term for banishment or "being forbidden to enter" is "dekin". The second Kanji, "forbid", is also seen on signage in various places in Japan. The placard for "no smoking" uses the second Kanji, "forbid".

Look at the two trees in the Kanji for "forbid". Could these trees refer to the tree of the knowledge of good and evil and the tree of life that were in the garden of Eden?

The first time mankind is ever banished is after they disobeyed God. They had previously been forbidden from eating of the tree of the knowledge of good and evil and now they were forbidden from eating of the tree of life.

outside　　forbid

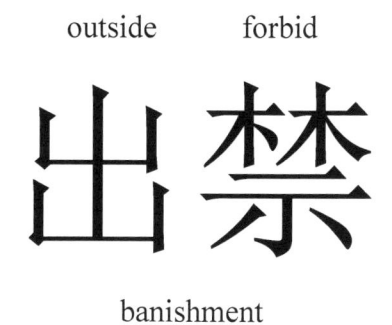

# 出禁

banishment

出 outside

木 tree

木 tree

示 show, point out

Adam and Eve not only experienced a spiritual separation from God, but a physical one.

They were no longer invited to come and rest and partake of the fruit of the tree of Life lest they should live forever, but were sent out with their heavy burden and a figurative "veil" came between God and man in the form of literal cherubim and a flaming sword keeping man from the Tree of Life and later as an actual veil in the Old Testament tabernacle, that God showed Moses the pattern for 1,500 years later.

What must it have been like to see the cherubim with the flaming sword guarding the tree of life?

For a thousand years outside the garden, man became incredibly evil,

> "The Lord saw that the wickedness of man was great in the earth, and that every intention of the thoughts of his heart was only evil continually. And the Lord regretted that he had made man on the earth, and it grieved him to his heart. So the Lord said, "I will blot out man whom I have created from the face of the land, man and animals and creeping things and birds of the heavens, for I am sorry that I have made them." But Noah found favor in the eyes of the Lord." (Genesis 6:5-8)

After God had created the heavens and the earth and everything in it, we are now at this awful place in the biblical record. What a sad picture we have of the state of man at this time.

Then God commanded Noah to build an ark and God destroyed all mankind and all the animals and birds, that were not safely in the Ark, in a worldwide flood.

If this is the judgment of God on mankind back then, how shall people who walk in disobedience today escape the wrath of God as it says in Colossians 3?

> *"On account of these the wrath of God is coming. In these you too once walked, when you were living in them."*
> *(Colossians 3:6, 7)*

This is why they need a preacher so that they can hear the good news and turn to God.

We've now come full circle back to our opening chapter where we saw the descendants after the flood dispersed around the world with their new languages given by God.

We've seen a context for man in the narrative of the Bible from creation to disobedience to destruction and confusion and now we will take a closer look at what man lost and what God's provision for man is.

## Chapter 7: Peeking through the Veil

WHEN GOD instructed the children of Israel to build the tabernacle, He gave them a design that separated man from the Holy of Holies, a room in which God dwelt, that was protected by a large veil. Mankind could not freely enter the Holy of Holies. This veil represented the flaming sword that guarded the entry to the garden where the Tree of Life was and it kept sinful man from the one and only Holy God.

God even gave explicit instructions to Moses regarding violations,

> *"and the Lord said to Moses, 'Tell Aaron your brother not to come at any time into the Holy Place inside the veil, before the mercy seat that is on the ark, so that he may not die. For I will appear in the cloud over the mercy seat.'" (Leviticus 16:2)*

God had created the Garden of Eden and placed Adam and Eve in it to work it and take care of it. After work, in the cool of the day, they would rest from their work in the Garden. This is how it should have remained. The character for "rest" has two parts, "person" and "tree."

*Note: Whenever the character for "person" is placed to the left side in any Kanji, the shape of the symbol generally has a more vertical look ( 亻 ) as seen in the Kanji for rest.*

A person standing next to the tree is the word for rest. We all may be able to relate to the picture of a person in the shade of a tree after working out in the sun all day. That picture fits pretty well with what is depicted in the Kanji for rest. But I want to take a little deeper look into the meaning of this character as it relates to rest in God's kingdom, and I think you'll agree that there is so much more to this picture than just a person standing next to any old tree.

休

rest

亻

person

木

tree

When man disobeyed God and ate from the tree of the knowledge of good and evil, God cast them out of the garden.

There was a physical wall of a flaming sword blocking the way to the tree of Life and a symbolic wall that was put up between man and God in the form of a veil, in the tabernacle. Mankind had no access to the tree of Life.

In the Old Testament, God gave the Israelites the plans for the tabernacle which included a veil that was placed between the area that man could enter and the Holy of Holies, where God resided.

Let's just picture an imaginary veil coming down and splitting the character for rest in half with man on one side and the tree on the other. The character for rest with a veil in the middle of it would look like this...

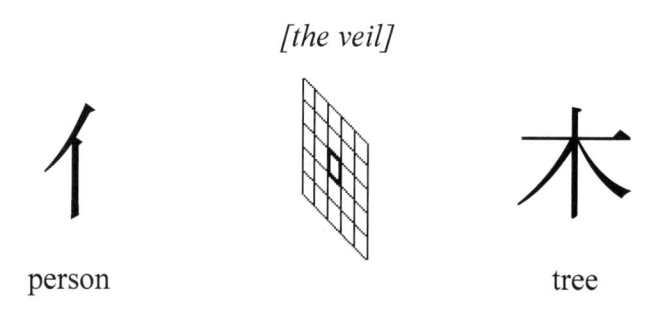

[the veil]

亻 　 　 木

person 　 　 tree

Imagine for a moment, that you are the person in the Kanji for rest with the veil separating you from the tree.

If you got up close and could peer through one of the tiny squares formed by the threads of the woven fabric you would see a tree enclosed within the borders of a square.

困

trouble

This is exactly what you would be looking at. The Kanji for "trouble" is an enclosed tree. Man knowing that he was not permitted access to the tree of Life would for the first time in history find himself in trouble. But man doesn't really realize from his perspective to what degree he is in trouble.

And if one were able to look through the tiny squares in the fabric of the veil from the point of view of the Tree of Life, which is God's point of view, you would see a...

囚

criminal

This is how God sees man. Man is a criminal in captivity awaiting judgment. And the sentence is death.

*"but of the tree of the knowledge of good and evil you shall not eat, for in the day that you eat of it you shall surely die."*
*(Genesis 2:17)*

Man became a prisoner and only God has the solution for setting the captives free. The word for prisoner in Japanese is made up of two Kanji, "criminal" and "person".

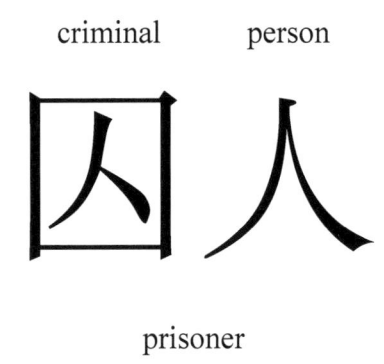

criminal　　person

囚人

prisoner

When man lost access to the Tree of Life, man became condemned, just as God had said, "You shall surely die." Man lost that rest that God had intended for him.

God made man with rest in mind. The fact that God commands man to keep the Sabbath (a day of rest) as one of the Ten Commandments,

*"Remember the Sabbath day, to keep it holy."*
*(Exodus 20:8)*

The significance of the Sabbath is not only that we should rest on the seventh day, but it is a weekly reminder (to remember) that this was the provision of rest that God intended for us in the garden of Eden beside the Tree of Life.

> *"For in six days the Lord made heaven and earth, the sea, and all that is in them, and rested on the seventh day. Therefore the Lord blessed the Sabbath day and made it holy." (Exodus 20:11)*

But we shouldn't give up hope, because God gives us this weekly rest as a reminder that he has provided the solution to restore the rest that we have been separated from.

Let's take a look at the next Kanji, "burden," in our verse,

> *"Come to me, all who labor and are heavy laden, and I will give you rest."*
> *(Matthew 11:28)*

# Chapter 8: The Burden that Man Carries

THE MOMENT Adam and Eve chose to disobey God, everything changed. Their relationship with God changed. Their eyes were opened to see both good and evil and they were burdened by this knowledge and by the guilt of their wrong doing. Their bodies began to die. And they knew that they had disobeyed God...

> *"And they heard the sound of the Lord God walking in the garden in the cool of the day, and the man and his wife hid themselves from the presence of the Lord God among the trees of the garden. But the Lord God called to the man and said to him, 'Where are you?'" (Genesis 3:8)*

荷

burden

The first time in recorded history that man bears a burden two things happen. The first is that the length of a man's life instantly becomes like the grass of the field. As God had said,

> *"...you shall surely die." (Genesis 2:17c)*

The second is that God calls out to the man and the woman with questions. They heard God ask them,

"...Where are you?" (Genesis 3:9)

"He said, 'Who told you that you were naked? Have you eaten of the tree of which I commanded you not to eat?'"
(Genesis 3:11)

"What is this that you have done?"
(Genesis 3:13)

We are now brought to the second of the four main Kanji in the passage from Matthew 11:28-30. The Kanji for "burden" is filled with interesting symbols.

人　荷　來　休
person　burden　come　rest

The first symbol is the symbol for grass. The grass is a reminder of the fragility of man's life. Since the day Adam and Eve ate of the tree of the knowledge of good and evil, all men and women eventually die. This was not what God intended when he created man.

⊢⊢⊦

grass

Modern man employs science to extend a few years of his life through regeneration, organ transplants and repair, even so,

> *"As for man, his days are like grass; he flourishes like a flower of the field; for the wind passes over it, and it is gone, and its place knows it no more." (Psalm 103:15, 16)*

> *"The grass withers, the flower fades: but the word of our God shall stand forever." (Isaiah 40:8)*

Man fades away, but God's Word endures forever. It's God's Word that tells us what our condition is and we come to know we are condemned, but it's also God's Word that declares God's provision for mankind, a way of salvation.

# 荷

burden

## 艹

grass

## 何

what

The next symbol is the Kanji for the word "what," and in Japanese it is the root for the other questions, where, why, when and how. It's these questions that barrage us as sinners.

何

what

It is the shame we are faced with as we anticipate the questions that will be asked. There are very few condemned men who have come to their senses that have not first had remorse as they contemplate these questions. And here are a few...

What have you done?

Where can you hide?

Why did you do it?

God's questions, though, lead us to understand that we have sinned. The answer is repentance.

A person must either acknowledge their wrongdoing and repent or they will find themselves carrying the uncomfortable weight of the burden of their sin.

何 　　　what

何処 　　where

如何 　　why

何時 　　when

如何 　　how

But wait a minute. Why isn't the word for burden the symbol of a donkey carrying a load of wood or something? You know, like "the beast of burden…"

Are we sure that this burden relates to man? There are other things that carry burdens.

Well, let's take a closer look at this Kanji and see what we come up with. If we look at the Kanji from a different perspective, and look very closely, we can see the symbol of "man" in the bottom left side.

Are the symbols next to this shape of the symbol of "man" an actual Kanji on its own? In all likelihood it might be, but maybe it's a symbol that would be meaningless. When we remove the symbol for man, we are indeed left with the Kanji for "torment".

The Kanji for burden shows that it is man who is burdened and not a donkey and look how overwhelming the torment is. It hovers over the person so that they are almost lost in it. Man is tormented by what he has done.

The reality is that the burdens of the whole world are the result of the sin of man.

> *"Therefore, just as sin came into the world through one man, and death through sin, and so death spread to all men because all sinned—"*
> *(Romans 5:12)*

It's man's fault. And that is why it is man that is at the center of the gospel message. But God has a solution for us.

# 荷

burden

# 亻

person, man

# 苛

torment

# Chapter 9: Thy Kingdom Come

EARLY IN Jesus' ministry the disciples had asked Him, "Lord, how should we pray? Teach us to pray." And Jesus responded with the prayer that many have committed to memory, the "Lord's Prayer".

> *"Our Father which art in heaven, Hallowed be Thy name. Thy kingdom come, Thy will be done on earth, as it is in heaven. Give us this day our daily bread. And forgive us our debts, as we forgive our debtors. And lead us not into temptation, but deliver us from evil. For Thine is the kingdom, and the power and glory, for ever. Amen."*
> *(Matthew 6:9-13, KJV)*

This would have been an appropriate prayer for the disciples to pray in preparation for and during that night in the garden of Gethsemane when Jesus would ask them to watch and pray. That the will of God would be done on earth, as it is in heaven.

> *"And going a little farther he fell on his face and prayed, saying, 'My Father, if it be possible, let this cup pass from me; nevertheless, not as I will, but as you will.'" (Matthew 26:39)*

Jesus goes back to His disciples in the garden finding them all asleep and asks them to keep watching and praying...

> *"Watch and pray that you may not enter into temptation. The spirit indeed is willing, but the flesh is weak." (Matthew 26:41)*

It is this prayer request to God that made sure God's kingdom would come and that God's will would be done and that Jesus would be put on the cross instead of us so that we would be forgiven our debts and not be led into temptation but we'd be delivered from the evil one...

Saint John on the Island of Patmos has a vision in Revelation chapter 5:1-10.

> *"Then I saw in the right hand of him who was seated on the throne a scroll written within and on the back, sealed with seven seals. And I saw a mighty angel proclaiming with a loud voice, "Who is worthy to open the scroll and break its seals?" And no one in heaven or on earth or under the earth was able to open the scroll or to look into it, and I began to weep loudly because no one was found worthy to open the scroll or to look into it. And one of the elders said to me, 'Weep no more; behold, the Lion of the tribe of Judah, the Root of David, has conquered, so that he can open the scroll and its seven seals.' And between the throne and the four living creatures and among the elders I*

*saw a Lamb standing, as though it had been slain, with seven horns and with seven eyes, which are the seven spirits of God sent out into all the earth. And he went and took the scroll from the right hand of him who was seated on the throne. And when he had taken the scroll, the four living creatures and the twenty-four elders fell down before the Lamb, each holding a harp, and golden bowls full of incense, which are the prayers of the saints. And they sang a new song, saying, 'Worthy are you to take the scroll and to open its seals, for you were slain, and by your blood you ransomed people for God from every tribe and language and people and nation, and you have made them a kingdom and priests to our God, and they shall reign on the earth.'"*

At what point are we invited into the kingdom? When Christ died on the cross. Without Christ's death on the cross there is no kingdom.

*"And they sang a new song, saying, 'Worthy are you to take the scroll and to open its seals, for you were slain, and by your blood you ransomed people for God from every tribe and language and people and nation, and you have made them a kingdom and priests to our God, and they shall reign on the earth.'" (Revelation 5:9-10)*

Thy kingdom come… but who are those that are purchased for God? They are only those who come to Christ.

*"Come to me, all who labor and are heavy laden, and I will give you rest."*
*(Matthew 11:28)*

Now we've come to the third Kanji in our list. The Kanji for the word, "come".

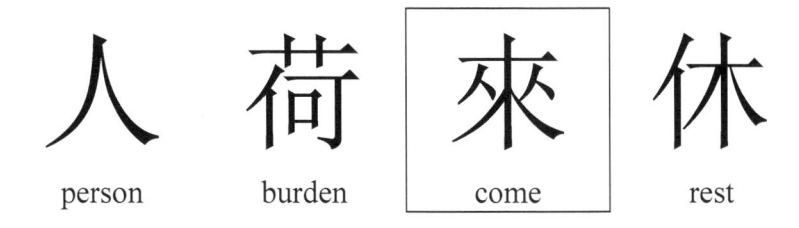

| 人 | 荷 | 來 | 休 |
|---|---|---|---|
| person | burden | come | rest |

*Note: The Kanji for "come" that I have chosen to use here is the version that was used before the war. It has since been changed to the following:*

来

come, *[post war simplified version]*

There may have been a specific reason for the decision to change the Kanji to what it is today. But I don't know what it is, other than the authors of the new version have gotten rid of the clear picture that I describe as follows.

You can probably now identify the symbols in the pre-war Kanji that I am using here. How many people are there in this Kanji?

There are three. There are two smaller people on either side of the larger person on the cross. The Bible gives us a detailed account of the crucifixion of Jesus. Jesus was crucified between two thieves.

> *"Then two robbers were crucified with him, one on the right and one on the left." (Matthew 27:38)*

These two "smaller" people on either side of the person on the cross represent the finality of man. That we will all die, physically. It is inescapable. But our eternal destination, on the other side of physical death, is based on a gift freely given and our choice to accept it or not.

The two destinations are to either enter into God's kingdom in heaven or to perish in hell separated from a holy God. Our choice, to accept this gift or not, determines our destination.

> *"For the wages of sin is death, but the free gift of God is eternal life in Christ Jesus our Lord." (Romans 6:23)*

來

come

人

person, man

十

complete, *[the cross]*

*Very important note: Stroke order is important when writing Kanji. In the case of the Kanji for "come," we do not write the symbol for "tree" first as you would expect. The order in which this Kanji is written is the horizontal crossbar, then the two smaller people, then the vertical pole, and finally the person on the cross.*

We have already seen that through man's disobedience to God we are deserving of death. But God has made a way for us to be restored to Him and His kingdom through the perfect sacrifice of His Son, Jesus Christ. This perfect sacrifice is sufficient to pay the debt that all mankind owe God.

Jesus' sacrifice on the cross is a free gift to all mankind. All we need to do is admit that we are sinners, deserving death, and to choose to accept God's free gift offered us through Christ Jesus.

We actually have a recorded transcript of the dialog between the two thieves and Jesus, each on their own crosses, that succinctly shows us the gift and the choice we have. Here it is,

> *"One of the criminals who were hanged railed at him saying, 'Are you not the Christ? Save yourself and us!' But the other rebuked him, saying, 'Do you not fear God, since you are under the same sentence of condemnation? And we indeed justly, for we are receiving the due reward of our deeds; but this man has done nothing wrong.' And he said, 'Jesus, remember me when you come into your kingdom.' And he said to him, 'Truly, I say to you, today you will be with me in Paradise.'" (Luke 23:39-43)*

At the crucifixion of Christ, two thieves were sentenced with him, one on his left and one on his right. They are both deserving of their punishment, yet the first thief in anger hurls insults and the other recognizes the sacrifice Jesus makes for all mankind.

The simple recognition of his own sin and of Christ's perfect sacrifice changes the second thief's eternal destination. Both thieves die, but one ends up separated from God and His kingdom and the other is united with God. This choice is available to all people in every nation. People in this world will go one way or the other.

While the Kanji are pictures, and a "picture is worth a thousand words", what exactly are those words? I believe the words for these pictures are found in the Bible, but how will the Japanese rediscover these words?

> *"How then will they call on him in whom they have not believed? And how are they to believe in him of whom they have never heard? And how are they to hear without someone preaching? And how are they to preach unless they are sent? As it is written, 'How beautiful are the feet of those who preach the good news!'" (Romans 10:14-15)*

On the surface, the world's problems seem so benign. With a close look at the Kanji for "world" you see the seriousness of the choice mankind has to make in light of the biblical record we have been investigating.

The Kanji for "world" is an intriguing picture. It is made up of three crosses. Two of the crosses are joined together (the center one and the one on the right) but the left one goes off on its own.

The telling thing about the cross on the left is that it terminates on the same path that the Kanji for "perish" does.

If people do not know the message, they will perish. If people hear the message and reject it, they will perish.

You should be able to see now how important it is to get the Gospel message out not only to the Japanese, but to the whole world.

世

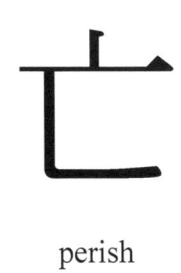

world


亡

perish

By the way, the word for "cross" in Japanese is "jyuujika", which simply means, "a stand in the shape of the number 10."

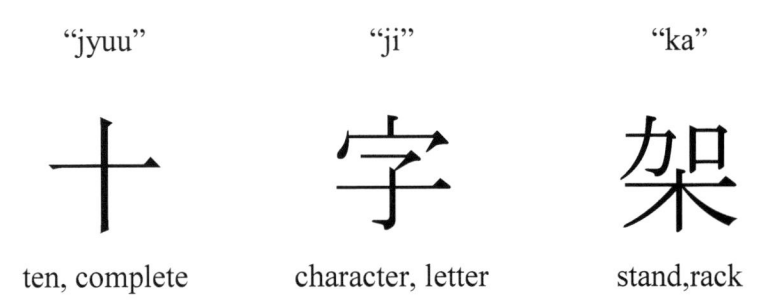

| "jyuu" | "ji" | "ka" |
|:---:|:---:|:---:|
| 十 | 字 | 架 |
| ten, complete | character, letter | stand, rack |

The symbol that looks like a cross is the number ten in Japanese and it also carries with it the meaning "complete". As in the word "enough" or "sufficient", which in Japanese looks like this,

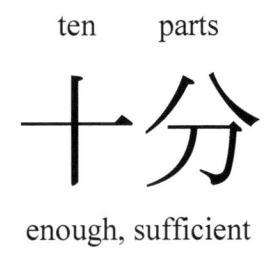

ten   parts

十分

enough, sufficient

Note: Jesus said, "it is finished" (complete) just before he died on the cross.

> *"When Jesus had received the sour wine, he said, "It is finished," and he bowed his head and gave up his spirit." (John 19:30)*

It is on the cross that Christ is crucified between two criminals and it is here that full payment for mankind is made. It is complete and it is the place we come to have our burden removed.

In John Bunyan's Pilgrim's Progress, Pilgrim's burden is removed at the cross. It is only here at the cross that we are freed from our burden.

This Kanji for "come" gives new meaning to the Christmas hymns,

> *"O come let us adore Him"*

And

> *"Joy to the world the LORD is come"*

When the shepherds come to Him and worship Him as the Christ child, they may have been unaware as to what it has cost Him to leave heaven and come to earth. He will grow up and face the cross where we all come to Him to bow down and worship Him as the Lamb that was slain to bring joy to the world.

## Chapter 10: Invitation to Rest

FINALLY WE return to look again at the word for "rest", the last Kanji in our list of four Kanji. When Christ died on the cross, the veil in the temple was torn in two from top to bottom.

> *"And behold, the curtain of the temple was torn in two, from top to bottom. And the earth shook, and the rocks were split."*
> *(Matthew 27:51)*

Man could now approach God through His Son Jesus Christ. The Kanji for man in "trouble" and man as a "captive" are only a condition that man chooses to remain in, because God has now made a way for all men to be free.

囚　　　　　　　　困

criminal　　　　　　trouble

Jesus opened the book of Isaiah and found the place where it was written,

"And the scroll of the prophet Isaiah was given to him. He unrolled the scroll and found the place where it was written, 'The Spirit of the Lord is upon me, because he has anointed me to proclaim good news to the poor. He has sent me to proclaim liberty to the captives and recovering of sight to the blind, to set at liberty those who are oppressed, to proclaim the year of the Lord's favor.'" (Luke 4:17-19)

"For there is one God, and there is one mediator between God and men, the man Christ Jesus, who gave himself as a ransom for all, which is the testimony given at the proper time."
(1 Timothy 2:5, 6)

| 人 | 荷 | 來 | 休 |
|---|---|---|---|
| person | burden | come | rest |

"Come to me, all who labor and are heavy laden, and I will give you rest."
(Matthew 11:28)

A person who realizes the burden of their own sin comes to the cross and finds rest. Man finds rest from the imposed burdens of traditions and the condemnation by the law, when they come to the cross of Christ.

> *"Cast your burden on the Lord and He will sustain you; he will never permit the righteous to be moved." (Psalm 55:22)*

I think you can see now that the word for rest appears to have more than just one person in it. Yes, certainly we can see the person standing by the tree.

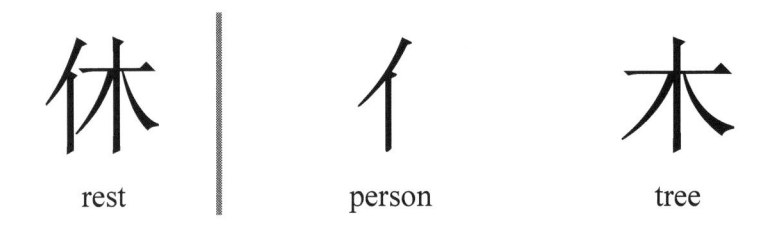

| 休 | 亻 | 木 |
|:---:|:---:|:---:|
| rest | person | tree |

But now we can see the second person in the Kanji for tree who appears to be on a cross, just like we saw Him in the Kanji for the word, "come" in the previous chapter.

*Note: I am taking interpretive license here. The Kanji for tree is never reduced into the parts (the cross, person) as I am showing. The Tree of Life likewise was never supposed to have a man hanging from a cross, but that is what Jesus' death on the cross means to all mankind, Life. And somehow the symbol for tree looks a lot like a man hanging on a cross.*

木

tree

十

complete, *[the cross]*

人

person, man

It is incomprehensible to put a man on a cross. Why would a man be placed on a cross, anyway? And why would I even suggest that? It sounds like foolishness.

> *"But we preach Christ crucified, unto the Jews a stumbling block, and unto the Greeks foolishness;"*
> *(1 Corinthians 1:23, KJV)*

But is it foolishness? From the Biblical account, we remember three famous trees, the tree of life, the tree of the knowledge of good and evil, and the tree that Jesus was nailed to. This third tree was the cross upon which the Romans hung Jesus and where he died. Because of man's sin by eating from the second tree, the tree of the knowledge of good and evil, man was barred from eating of the first tree, the tree of life, lest he live forever.

The gospel teaches that it was Jesus' self sacrifice, allowing Himself to be killed, being nailed to the cross (a tree) which has given mankind restored access to eternal life, our "tree of life", what a fitting symbol for tree.

The Chinese symbol for tree above was set in stone long before the Romans began practicing crucifixion. But I want you to see one more Chinese character that has an extraordinary concurrence of symbols and meaning that also would have biblical reference in light of my interpretation expressed above. The Kanji is the word for "thorn".

What we see here is the Kanji for tree and a symbol in the shape of an "upside-down box" in the middle of it. The position of this symbol on the "tree" Kanji is highlighting the exact location where the thorns would be on the person who wore them on the cross.

束

thorn

木

tree

冂

upside-down box

Satan plotted evil, but God's plan turned it into good. The following Kanji has the meaning "plot" and "plan" and take a look at what it looks like.

From Satan's perspective, the cross was a plot to have mankind kill the Son of God. But God's plan was for salvation through His Son's death so that the world has a way back to God. What Satan meant for evil, God planned for good for all of us.

The Bible records the story of Joseph who became second to the Pharaoh in Egypt. His brothers had sold him to slave traders in his youth. Joseph endured much hardship in Egypt as a prisoner, but in God's timing, God made Joseph the most powerful man in Egypt next to Pharaoh. When Joseph finally meets his brothers years later, he forgives them saying,

> *"As for you, you meant evil against me, but God meant it for good, to bring it about that many people should be kept alive, as they are today."*
> *(Genesis 50:20)*

This statement is a picture of what Jesus did for us, even though we meant Him harm when we nailed Him to the cross.

> *"And Jesus said, 'Father, forgive them, for they know not what they do.' And they cast lots to divide his garments." (Luke 23:34)*

計

plot, plan

言

to say

十

complete, *[the cross]*

# Chapter 11: He is Our Righteousness

THERE IS one more Kanji that we need to look at since it's an important part of Biblical history that we have been looking at. The Kanji is the word for "righteousness".

義

righteousness

Remember when we were looking at the Kanji for "sacrifice", (in Chapter 2), we said that we'd come back to address the real meaning of "the executioner", with its parts, "hand" and "spear"?

犠

sacrifice

Well, that Kanji is really the word for "me".

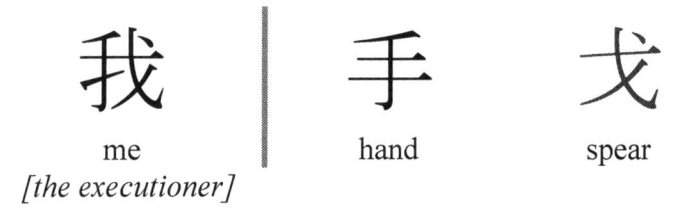

| 我 | 手 | 戈 |
|---|---|---|
| me | hand | spear |
| [the executioner] | | |

It was for me that Christ was crucified. Jesus is the slain Lamb of God who bought me with His blood. The song sung in heaven about the slain Lamb of God says,

> *"And they sang a new song, saying, 'Worthy are you [Jesus] to take the scroll and to open its seals, for you were slain, and by your blood you ransomed people for God from every tribe and language and people and nation,'"*
> *(Revelation 5:9)*

Let's look at how the word for lamb, in the Kanji for "righteousness", is drawn. Notice that it is missing the tail. If I were to ask any elementary student in Japan what this symbol in the Kanji for sheep represents here, what do you suppose they would see?

Wool?

The body of a lamb?

Its legs?

The rib cage?

義

righteousness

羊   sheep, lamb

我   me

They would tell you that they see a "king".

$$王$$

king

And in the Kanji for righteousness there are two diagonal strokes on top of the king.

It is interesting to note that yes, while these markings are commonly referred to as the horns of the sheep, these two strokes do not exist on the Kanji for other horned animals such as oxen and deer or any other.

丶 丿

Not all sheep have horns, but there is a lamb that does.

> *"And between the throne and the four living creatures and among the elders I saw a Lamb standing, as though it had been slain, with seven horns and with seven eyes, which are the seven spirits of God sent out into all the earth." (Revelation 5:6)*

There are over 400 Kanji in Japanese that use these two stroke markings and not one is interpreted as horns, except here in the Kanji for sheep. In Japanese and Chinese, these strokes are in the "crown" position in the Kanji and they have the actual meaning, "to put together". For our purposes, we will use these as the mnemonic for "horns" in the scripture above and as a crown of "thorns".

Throughout Old Testament biblical prophecy, there is an important message,

> *"In his days Judah will be saved, and Israel will dwell securely. And this is the name by which he will be called: 'The Lord is our righteousness.'"*
> *(Jeremiah 23:6)*

which was not just a title, but a God mandated event that had to occur as it was prophesied,

> *"...like a lamb that is led to the slaughter..."*
> *(Isaiah 53:7b)*

> *"...he poured out his soul to death and was numbered with the transgressors..."*
> *(Isaiah 53:12b)*

> *"...so that, when they look on me, on him whom they have pierced..."*
> *(Zechariah 12:10b)*

> "they shall come and proclaim his righteousness to a people yet unborn, that he has done it."
> (Psalm 22:31)

One week prior to Christ's crucifixion the people of Jerusalem took branches of the palm trees and went out to meet Him and they began shouting,

> "So they took branches of palm trees and went out to meet him, crying out, 'Hosanna! Blessed is he who comes in the name of the Lord, even the King of Israel!'"
> (John 12:13)

There is a particular slice in time at the crucifixion of Christ that is depicted in this Chinese character for righteousness. Jesus is nailed to the cross with a crown of thorns on his head with the inscription, "King of the Jews" above him, and he says, "It is finished" as he takes his last breath. The soldier pierces his side with the spear and the centurion declares,

> "Now when the centurion saw what was done, he glorified God, saying, Certainly this was a righteous man." (Luke 23:47, KJV)

義

righteousness

丶丿

"...and twisting together a crown of thorns, they put it on him."
(Mark 15:17)

王

"And they began to salute him, 'Hail, King of the Jews!'" (Mark 15:18)

羊

"...Behold, the Lamb of God, who takes away the sin of the world!" (John 1:29)

"...*a Lamb standing, as if slain, with seven horns ...*" (Revelation 5:6b)

我

"... we (我我) are receiving the due reward of our deeds; but this man has done nothing wrong. And he said, 'Jesus, remember me (我) when you come into your kingdom!'" (Luke 23:41b,42)

戈

"But one of the soldiers pierced his side with a spear, and at once there came out blood and water." (John 19:34)

義

"Now when the centurion saw what was done, he glorified God, saying, Certainly this was a righteous man."
(Luke 23:47, KJV)

> *"Therefore, we are ambassadors for Christ, God making his appeal through us. We implore you on behalf of Christ, be reconciled to God. For our sake he made him to be sin who knew no sin, so that in him we might become the righteousness of God."*
> *(2 Corinthians 5:20, 21)*

Each one of us becomes intimately aware of our own sins when we stand at the cross. It is very personal. We begin to realize that we are the ones who had Him killed. It was for us.

To illustrate that he died for all of us, write the word for "us" in Japanese, (我我) "wareware". The use of the word, 我 "ware" for "me" when repeated creates the word "us" or "we" in Japanese. This is as if to say corporately, "Christ died for me, too."

Though Jesus Christ died on the cross, He rose again after three days just as He said,

> *"for he was teaching his disciples, saying to them, 'The Son of Man is going to be delivered into the hands of men, and they will kill him. And when he is killed, after three days he will rise.'"*
> *(Mark 9:31)*

Jesus Christ is this "Son of Man".

Remember that Japanese phrase we looked at in chapter 6 meaning "to decay completely"?

朽ち果てる

The above phrase is a picture of what started the whole downfall of mankind. It is a picture described in Romans 5:12,

> *"Therefore, just as sin came into the world through one man, and death through sin, and so death spread to all men because all sinned—"*

We know the story of the garden of Eden. We know that man disobeyed God and ate the fruit and God had to enclose the tree of Life to keep man from accessing it and living for ever. And because we are all of Adam, we all sinned. And because of sin, we all die.

It is a picture of access to the tree of Life being closed off to man and we all die and decay.

$$朽$$

decay

Because man sinned against God and ate the fruit of the tree of the knowledge of good and evil believing he would be enlightened.

$$果$$

fruit, to die, "enlightenment"

This is the picture of all men for thousands of years from the garden of Eden and even into today. Sinful man simply undergoes decay.

This is the very phrase that is used in the following Scripture in the Japanese translation of the Bible that says Jesus did not undergo decay:

> *"And we preach to you the good news of the promise made to the fathers, that God has fulfilled this promise to our children in that He raised up Jesus, as it is also written in the second Psalm, 'YOU ARE MY SON, TODAY I HAVE BEGOTTEN YOU.' As for the fact that He raised Him up from the dead, no longer to return to decay, He has spoken in this way: 'I WILL GIVE YOU THE HOLY and SURE blessings OF DAVID.' Therefore He also says in another Psalm, 'YOU WILL NOT ALLOW YOUR HOLY ONE TO UNDERGO DECAY.' For David, after he had served the purpose of God in his own generation, fell asleep, and was laid among his fathers and underwent decay; but He whom God raised did not undergo decay. Therefore let it be known to you, brethren, that through Him forgiveness of sins is proclaimed to you, and through Him everyone who believes is freed from all things, from which you could not be freed through the Law of Moses"*
> (Acts 13:32-39, New American Standard Bible)

In this verse, we clearly see, that though every man does in fact die and decay as David did, Jesus Christ who died on the cross was raised from the dead and did not undergo decay.

That very death and decay that God told Adam and Eve would be the result of their sin of eating the fruit of the knowledge of good and evil in the garden of Eden is conquered by Jesus Christ. Jesus put an end to our separation from God.

*"Therefore, brothers, since we have confidence to enter the holy places by the blood of Jesus, by the new and living way that he opened for us through the curtain, that is, through his flesh,"*
*(Hebrews 10:19b,20)*

Jesus Christ is risen!

## Conclusion: The Crossroad

AT THE beginning of this book I had stated that the symbols for man represent specific people, both historical and present-day figures within the context of the biblical narrative.

| 人 | 荷 | 來 | 休 |
|---|---|---|---|
| person | burden | come | rest |

The symbol for person in our first two Kanji represents all mankind. Those people who still carry the heavy burden that Christ magnanimously wants to remove, whether they've come to recognize their burdened state or not.

The third Kanji represents three historical people, Christ Himself on the cross and, on either side of Him, the two criminals at Calvary.

The fourth and final Kanji represents all people who come to Jesus Christ and are freed from their burden of sin.

> "He himself bore our sins in his body on the tree, that we might die to sin and live to righteousness. By his wounds you have been healed."
> (1 Peter 2:24a)

> *"who gave himself for us to redeem us from all lawlessness and to purify for himself a people for his own possession who are zealous for good works."*
> *(Titus 2:14)*

These good deeds are not burdensome man-pleasing rituals. Jesus encourages us with these words:

> *"Take my yoke upon you, and learn from me, for I am gentle and lowly in heart, and you will find rest for your souls. For my yoke is easy, and my burden is light."*
> *(Matthew 11:29-30)*

庠

school

A Kanji for the word, "school", has the symbol for lamb or sheep in it. It is a good reminder that we need to learn from the Lamb of God. Well, if we are to "go to school" and learn from the Lamb, what is the curriculum He gives us?

It is the Word of God.

As we read His Word and "learn of Him," we will find rest for our souls.

Because God gives us a choice, we stand at a crossroads.

How will you walk out your life? God has provided the path for you. Will you take the path to the cross? Will you admit to your sin and will you come to Christ in repentance believing that He died for you? Will you come willing to learn from Him?

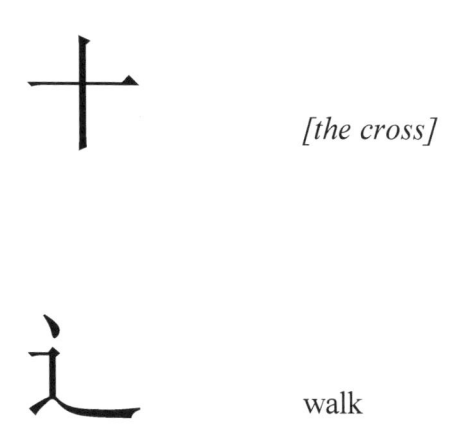

辻

crossroad

十   *[the cross]*

辶   walk

If you choose to come to Him, you will find rest for your soul.

If you're not sure how to pray, Jesus gives us a picture of what His Father is looking for.

Jesus tells us this parable in Luke 18:10-14,

> *"Two men went up into the temple to pray, one a Pharisee and the other a tax collector. The Pharisee, standing by himself, prayed thus: 'God, I thank you that I am not like other men, extortioners, unjust, adulterers, or even like this tax collector. I fast twice a week; I give tithes of all that I get.' But the tax collector, standing far off, would not even lift up his eyes to heaven, but beat his breast, saying, 'God, be merciful to me, a sinner!' I tell you, this man went down to his house justified, rather than the other. For everyone who exalts himself will be humbled, but the one who humbles himself will be exalted."*

We are told that,

> *"If we confess our sins, he is faithful and just to forgive us our sins and to cleanse us from all unrighteousness." (1 John 1:9)*

Amen.

# Appendix

The following diagram depicts the single path that all mankind take to find rest for their souls. 1) Man can follow the path that God has prepared through His Son by recognizing their condition before God and accepting Christ's sacrifice and be reconciled to God or 2) they can reject Christ, follow other religions and perish.

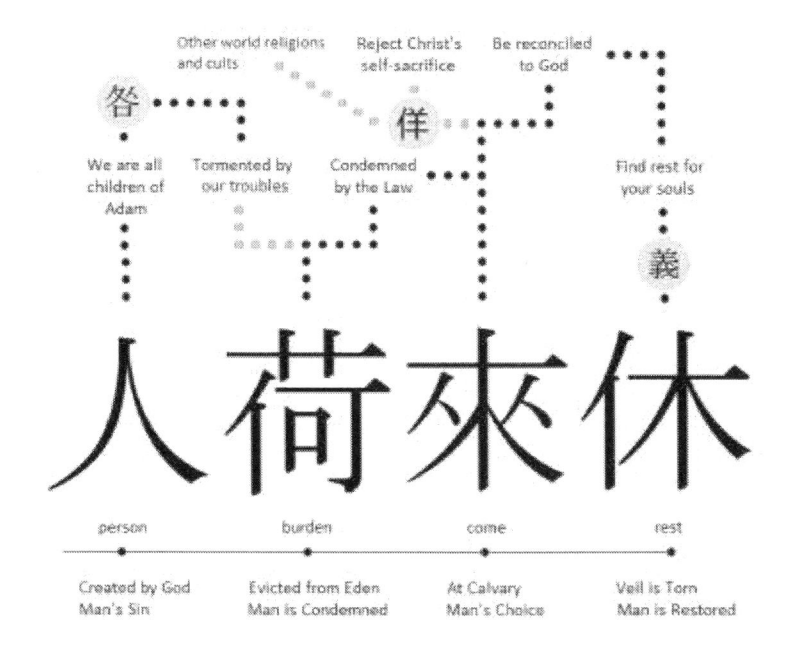

```
       Other world religions    Reject Christ's      Be reconciled
       and cults                self-sacrifice       to God

   咎                              伴

   We are all    Tormented by    Condemned           Find rest for
   children of   our troubles    by the Law          your souls
   Adam
                                                         義

   人            荷              來                   休

   person        burden          come                rest

   Created by God   Evicted from Eden   At Calvary        Veil is Torn
   Man's Sin        Man is Condemned    Man's Choice      Man is Restored
```

**Person**

Man and woman are created by God. (Genesis 1:27) The Man and the woman disobey God. (Genesis 3:6-8) The sin of Adam in the garden of Eden affects all mankind. (Romans 5:12)

## Burden

Adam and Eve are evicted from the garden of Eden. (Genesis 3:24) All mankind was condemned by the one transgression. (Romans 5:18) We know that we are sinners because of God's Law. (Romans 3:20)

## Come

Christ bore the burden of our sins in His body on the cross. (1 Peter 2:24) Man can choose to come to Jesus. (Matthew 11:28) The Veil that separates a holy God from sinful man is torn. (Matthew 27:51)

## Rest

Mankind can be restored to a right relationship with God. (2 Corinthians 5:20, 21)

# Notes

Made in the USA
Lexington, KY
23 April 2016